A PRECISE CHAOS

ARROWSMITH
PRESS

A Precise Chaos
Jo-Ann Mort

ISBN: 979-8-9904050-5-9

Library of Congress Control Number: 2024916744

Boston — New York — San Francisco — Baghdad
San Juan — Kyiv — Istanbul — Santiago, Chile
Beijing — Paris — London — Cairo — Madrid
Milan — Melbourne — Jerusalem — Darfur

11 Chestnut St.
Medford, MA 02155

arrowsmithpress@gmail.com
www.arrowsmithpress.com

The sixty-fourth Arrowsmith book
was typeset & designed by Ezra Fox
for Askold Melnyczuk & Alex Johnson
in EB Garamond

Cover Art: Wassily Kandinsky, *Black and Violet*, 1923.

A PRECISE CHAOS

Poems by Jo-Ann Mort

To the blessed memory of my parents
who always believed in my poetry

And to my first readers and dear friends for a collective 148 years—
Jenny Doctorow, Anita Glesta, and Brian Morton

CONTENTS

Oh, I have made myself a tribe
Out of my true affections,
And my tribe is scattered!

—*Stanley Kunitz, Layers*

The Men

The men were larger than life—
starting revolutions in their heads and in their classrooms,
negotiating contracts, whispering
into the ears of governors and presidents.

The men were larger than life,
so life eluded them: the quiet time, the simple sip,
the innocent glance, the hearth
and home. And I, too, it—life, eluded me.

The men were larger than life.
They were my life, my circle, my hearth, my home.
And then, the revolution failed, the workers lost
their jobs to China, and we all grew older.

The men were larger than life. They sparked
a room when they walked in, if not a revolution.
They were larger. They
left wives, and children, and me.

Life was larger than these men.
They meant well. They desired great change.
But life is larger than these men
and now, life is where I am.

In Mostar, City of Bridges

I recognize the hotel on the evening news.
You tell me the outdoor café
is now a mass grave, bodies piled on top of the patio
where I sat just a year ago, sipping cold beer served
by a waiter in a formal vest and bow tie.

> *Bullet holes through its corridors, its spine,*
> *its doorways. Windows shattered into the river flowing below*
> *until the river is a congested mixture of glass and blood,*
> *like a frozen crimson stream of broken ice in the middle of summer.*

All the cafés along the Neretva River are blown to pieces.
The red-headed Muslim woman who tended bar, cigarette in hand,
espresso cup empty by the ashtray, one gold hoop in her ear,
sleeveless black t-shirt; now, she is a refugee, or worse. . .
The Old Town, the Turkish Bridge (they will build it good as new, you predict).

One summer, we sipped beer by a river laced with minarets,
each thin tower extending like an arm waving its way through
delicate nature, these travelers from the 16th century.
These treacherous and beautiful mountains, their heated, sun-
drenched stone rising toward a sky that offers nothing.
A god, torn in so many pieces, he explodes across the countryside.

You've gone to find a part for your motorbike. I sip my beer.
Order another. You arrive in time to pay for it in dinars.
We walk together, past the begging Roma children and the political
posters that couldn't portend how the world will erupt
when civil politics becomes anathema.

Soon, we will drive to the ferry stop to return to the island.
Drink grappa hulled from the Dalmatian Coast. We stare silently at the clear water.
Relief boats. Mined harbors. Naval blockades. Body parts on the street splayed
like a child's forgotten play set. There's a stray leg, a finger.
The unclouded Adriatic, your tiny villa, your garden with lemons and rosemary,
the puny tangerines.

We finish our beer at the edge of the mass grave as we sit outside
the Grand Hotel. You tuck dinars beneath the beer mugs. We walk
arm in arm past the children. The spires rise through the flames.
Bullet holes turn their slender arms into sieves that ooze
out centuries of something that almost resembled civilization.

Market Day

Python belt on my jeans.
You bought it for me maybe
thirty years ago at the market
in Oaxaca, bargaining until the price
was on the floor. It still fits me,
wrapped around my stomach like
a safety belt that holds memories
close to my skin,
a binding or a soft kiss
each time I pull up my jeans.

"Doll," you called me, your
Serbian accent getting thicker
each year that you lived in America.
Once, you met me at the airport
in Mexico City, handing me
a canister of Mace pepper spray
to keep in my bag while we traveled.
But instead of using it against a bandit
or rapist, the cap got loose in the back pocket
of my jeans while the yellow liquid seeped
down my leg like the stripe on a wild animal.

I can still feel the burn, decades later.
Our immediate need was to find me
a new pair of jeans, so we shopped near
the Zocalo where the stores were full
of denim, but only for tiny Mexican bodies,
not my tall and angled bones. The pants
we bought were too short and too wide,
but the belt kept them firm around me.

I returned once to Mexico without you.
In the market in Cuernavaca, a vendor
weighed strands of sterling to sell me,
looped around my neck and chest,
heavy and light silver and the hoops,
costing a peso or two, threaded
through my ears.

You are dead. Your ashes
scattered over the Adriatic.
I remember the cut flowers
in the glass jar in your bedroom
on Brač, left for us by your daughter
for our return from Dubrovnik.
The put-put of your motorboat
as it crawled around the island.
We docked for fresh caught
smelts and hard crust bread
soaked in Dalmatian wine.

On market day, we would walk
down the steps of your street
to the dock where the produce
displayed was tomatoes and green
onions. It was a simpler time,
even though Tito was barely dead
and a civil war was bubbling
from the mountains and the fields.
I was young then, or at least
in my twenties, and thought I
had all the time in the world.

Tonight, the music near my house is live
as I sit with friends you never met
eating roasted salmon and drinking wine snuck
into the park in water bottles.
The belt is beneath my t-shirt.
I remember it only when my mind
wanders from the stage and not really in boredom,
but with a sort of reflex wanting the air
beside me to welcome you.

Paris

We visited the Louvre where at least one prince reeled in his own reverie. Trocadero, where you took my picture to freeze my love for you forever.

In a bar near the Odeon, we toasted your friends who lost wives and lovers to illness, madness, envy, or hate.

Then, at Orly, I sat for half the night grounded by fog, thinking should I call you or wait for your return a week later?

For you, it was 1968 all over again, when the cry of the students was a flaming brush on the charcoal sky, when you ran across Europe to stand at the barricades.

"I thought the Revolution had arrived," you confided over vodka and tears. But even then, there was your return ticket, the moments erupting into seconds of disarray.

All before the Gulag, Cambodia, tenure, child support. Before the 1980s made the entire world resemble a vast America that so gracelessly smothered desire.

Democracy in Autumn

On the Rue Saint-Jean, one red tree
glares at us. Says: summer is over.
We are ripening into winter.

After breakfast, we walk on the Plains of Abraham.
Like the heat, we are stuck out of season.
We have survived continents and break ups,
civil wars and revolutions.
You return to your former Yugoslavia
to organize a pro-democracy group.

A dozen horse-drawn carts assemble
on the street in the Old Town.
We walk hand in hand, despite everything.

Later, I watch this confused autumn
from my window in the hotel.
You are floors below me,
delivering a speech about workplace democracy.
We, who are so righteous.
Where does it lead us?

Snapshots from Brač

i.

A whole new geography here.
Day after day without rain.
The Dalmatian Coast is drowning in sun.
Terrace farming: armies of pebble
cluster in the countryside.
Organized rubble, they are the teeth
of mountains that bite into heaven.

ii.

The church bells ring every hour.
Widows of Christ traverse the pavements
in black sweaters, their dresses hang
near the ground. Black short stockings.
Their eyes look into emptiness
searching for the body of Christ.

iii.

There are no time clocks
on the workers' beach.
For one month, work
is a foreign language.
I hide behind your lace of Serbo-Croatian
or now, Croatian, as the language plays
games amid the civil war.

iv.

New York is the city you lean toward
but it is not your earth.
A friend of ours once said:
"You should die in your own language."
Your ashes skim the Adriatic
then join the clear, floating heaven.

For Tito and You

You brought me to Brač
with its market of tomatoes and green onions.
By boat and by land,
in your tiny red Yugo, you took my hand
promising me nothing and everything.
I believed all of it, the summer sun
along the hilltops, the tempered Adriatic,
actually existing socialism; but then,
tumbling like stones toppling,
there were ripped borders, villages,
the somnambulism erased and the
fires ignited. We tried

To love each other so many times.
But we could never find the formula.
The calm to lay over the turmoil.
Your cracked chest, like your cracked country.
You kept testing your heart, that worn
organ, looking for more and frantic
ways to love. There was no serenity
in our revolution. There was love,
but when was that ever enough?

In Taormina

Volcano tears that nurture robust wine,
chocolate from Modica, red Sicilian oranges
like the silt of flames. And then, the miles
of bleached-out fields, along the roadside
with lumps of rolled hay gathered here, gathered there.

This: there is advantage in a new landscape—
the silent fields, the river of dense lava
swimming clefts with decades; no, centuries of stories
to tell, now covered with litter and coffee lids.

"From out the dark door of the secret earth," Lawrence's snake
pulls his body first out—then, safely into a hole in creviced concrete.

Wildfires, the careless, selfish cigarette tossed outside a car
igniting miles of vegetation, shuttering the airport in Catania.
Along the highway, road signs shredded, blackened.

On the terrace of the Grand Hotel, lights at dusk
dance like moondust in the lap of Etna.
The Ionian Sea is the color of sky.
It's a puddle of calm tears; a pallet for the spewed ash.

Also Lawrence, his tortoise: "dumb and visionless."
This bold idiocy of people who obscure
the horizon they don't own.

Not in This Lifetime

My daughters will be named
Bella and Justice.
Their curly hair will be blondish brown
with ringlets gracing their shoulders
just like mine before I dyed it red.
When I am old, they will sing to me—
quietly, breathlessly, above sound,
above light.

And when my eyes go, they will read to me.
But mostly, they will do everything
that I forgot to do or simply
didn't get around to. They will change
the world or at least a tiny slice of it.
Wearing black on black like their mom,
they will shout, they will sing;
they will appear—just not
in this lifetime, or to me.

How She Remembers Him

1. Knatchbull, Summer Rain

    His wide, thick wrists. She doesn't remember these wrists from their meeting in Berlin. She remembers him, wrongly, as thin, even slight. His thick shoulders, too—she doesn't recall them either from their first time. The two moles on the back of his neck. His broad, possessing face.

    She wants darkness, total, complete. She wants to lose herself in sex with him, but she is too aware of him, of the light, of his ex-wife's propinquity, of the rain falling outside on Knatchbull, the summer rain of August. The temperature barely reaches 60 degrees Fahrenheit.

    He gets lost en route to Oxford. They drive in circles on the motorway. In Oxford, he shows her his college, the chapel where he sang in the choir with a choir master who introduced him to Harold Wilson. For him, the rest is history.

    The inevitable rain. They won't be able to walk along the river's edge or go punting. They drink tea under an umbrella. He apologizes for smoking. He tried a patch on his ass on the first day she arrived, but when it didn't work, he said, "Fuck it, I'm smoking." And he smoked.

2. She Wants to Make Phone Calls

She wants to make phone calls, to Israel, to Croatia (she wants to call it Yugoslavia), to London. Just a week ago, in Derbyshire. On the floor, on a mattress, under a duvet with S. He recoiled from public affection, at least that's how he explained it when she asked why he wouldn't let her touch him with others around them. "Your trouble is, you've got yourself a Brit," he said, as they placed their things in the middle bedroom of the old Derbyshire farmhouse.

Downstairs, the family was preparing dinner. There were furious phone calls back and forth about the mine closings. They were his oldest friends. She thought: "What the hell do I need this for and where the hell am I?"

She wants to call Jerusalem. She wants to speak to her friend Michal about the peace process. Arafat is coming to Jerusalem, or Jericho, or Gaza City. She wants to make long-distance calls.

In the morning, S. places his penis in the crack at the top of her legs. He grows hard and then he turns her toward him. "This is nice," he tells her. Downstairs, she can hear people moving in the house.

3. She Reads About Him

As they drive on the outskirts of Oxford, he tells her about a college girlfriend. "She wrote about me," he says as he points to the apartment they shared over 30 years ago. She looks him up in the college girlfriend's autobiography. He is unnamed, but it is obvious that it is him. She quickly dismisses the harsh comments as passion gone wrong from decades past. Later, she reconsiders her dismissal.

What will she write about him? He speaks to her in the third person as they drive along the Thames.

Each time she hears the third person interjection, she wonders: Does he see himself simply as a character she will create or as a character he has created?

4.   In Berlin, He Sings *Kindertotenlieder*

She meets him in Berlin. They sit together on the steps outside the main hall in the Reichstag. She wants to hear Gorbachev speak, but he doesn't and he infatuates her. So, she doesn't go inside; Gorbachev's Russian trails faintly in the background. She wears a black stretch mid-length skirt that was featured in the New York Times Magazine spring fashion pages, a tapered button-down denim shirt, and short black suede Clergerie boots with heavy black stockings. The skirt has an oversized copper zipper in the front from top to bottom.

In the 3-Star hotel on Lindenstrasse, they make love for the first time. He appears satisfied, but aggrieved, not at her, but at his ex-wife, his party, the world, Neil Kinnock.

He sings Mahler's *Kindertotenlieder* in the shower. The room is an apricot pink. No one in the hotel speaks English. He addresses everyone but her in German. In the morning, she watches him put his dirty sky-blue shirt in his suitcase and unwrap a clean shirt, the exact same style and color.

Later, in August, in his home on Knatchbull, he will show her his closet, stacked with the blue shirts from a tailor in Hong Kong. He says it is easier to dress that way, no need for decisions.

She remembers the tiny poetry of the talk and touch of affection, but also the alliteration of meso-economics and Maastricht and their first conversation—on the bus filled with ministerial staff and advisors off to Potsdam for cocktails and Bach. She is arguing with an Israeli friend about free trade, while she watches his lips begin to turn up in a smile. That night, he walks her to her hotel on Alexanderplatz, but her gay roommate will soon be home from the late-night clubs, so they turn away without going upstairs.

In the morning, in the apricot colored room, he puts on his blue shirt and she, her denim tapered top. He appears aggrieved, but not at her. He sings *Kindertotenlieder* and smokes.

Overnight

And then, in the deep night, the dew settled like a blanket
over our sleeping bags, sealing us into the flannel lining.
Our tummies were happy with the memory of s'mores—
the wilting, flaming marshmallows, sweet as they fell
off the knobby branches into our hands or on
to the shell of a graham cracker with chocolate melting
like a cap over the white meringue.

We were ten, eleven, somewhere before the steep climb
to adulthood. The stars were so dense that the sky looked
like a lattice sheath. For us, in the faux campground,
this was as far as the road carried us, untethered for one night
from the carpool station wagon, the cul-de-sacs where we lived,
in an America stretching away from the cities to build new frontiers
without imagination or exotica, just a framed sameness.

This was childhood—or what I want to remember—
the soft sky of nighttime, the frivolous expanse that spread
across Miquon and Spring Mill, near the creek outside of our bunks.
This one unordinary night, when the outdoors was all there was,
natural darkness with no walls, no windows, only the blanket of dew
dusting this universe of children—refugees from the suburbs—
half-asleep by the smoldering campfire.

With Allen Ginsberg in the Gymnasium

My first poetry reading was in the over-bright gymnasium
at Bucks County Community College. It was 1973.
Allen Ginsberg on a sofa with his leg in a cast,
the sofa on a riser near the basketball scoreboard.
Peter Orlovsky, behind him—a solo chorus with a lute.

In between chants and singing his poems,
Ginsberg welcomed his father Louis to read
his poetry in rhymed verse, wound as tight
as the son's verse was loose all over the page, snaking
and swirling the sounds of a century.

Louis wore a powder blue jacket and matching tie.
Allen's stepmother, Edith, sat in the bleachers, clutching her purse
like my Aunt Sarah used to do—as if all her earthly possessions
were stored in that little black box with a fake pearl handle.

I never knew her last name while she lived. Widowed,
she was just Aunt Sarah. After she died, my uncle
gave me her passport that he kept in a box of old photos.

Census forms from 1910, 1920, and 1930 list
my family from Austria, Germany, Poland, Russia, Ukraine.
But what did these borders matter?
There was really just one big landmass of dead Jews.
On my mother's side of the family, we have
only this passport, from Radechov, in Galicia.

Aunt Sarah with thick ankles
and lace up oxfords with raised heels, wire rim glasses,
house-coat dresses. Her apartment above the store smelled
like must and talcum powder.

One evening, I saw Allen Ginsberg
on First Avenue near St. Mark's. I was with Bogdan,
who knew him from the 1950s Village scene.
He looked lonely and out of place, even though
gentrification hadn't compressed the East Village
into every town USA just yet.
They nodded hello to each other,
compelled by the gentle whisper of acquaintance
that informs our lives as we age,
while the memories of our younger selves dance
on the corner without regard to anything
except the steps we take to find our way home.

Summer circa 1967-2xxx

My mother and the other ladies
lie prone in plastic
yellow and green lounge chairs
on our front lawn.
Tin foil reflectors emanate
from their necks like limbs.
Baby oil—smeared on their faces
and arms. They glow, glow, glow
in the humid sun.

They drink iced tea with lemon
and they don't work.
Doris, Sandy, Muriel, Peggy, Mildred.
They glow, glow, glow
in the humid sun.

In Ventnor, I lie
with my mother and Aunt Lily
on the hot freckles
of sand. My skin fries
to a lean red, like the hard
shell of a lobster.
My eyes puff up, nearly pasted shut.
Mom places tea bags on my crusted eyes,
sprays Solarcaine on my burnt skin.

"A sunburn will turn to tan
the next day," she counsels
me and herself; her skin,
leathery and lined before
she is 40. She still glows in the humid sun.

When the glow fades,
her skin, leathery and lined,
sags; her hunched shoulders
nearly hide her neck.

She visits me in Brooklyn,
walking slowly, tentative,
through my neighborhood
without lawns or lawn chairs
just a park where women, drenched in SPF 50,
sunbathe in the path of soccer balls.

She is wearing a baby-blue cardigan
buttoned up like a shirt.
The skin in the middle of her body
is still forgiving and supple,
with no lasting
exposure from the sun.

In the natural light
of my living room,
I examine her chin
to find three stray
dark hairs, dangling,
which I snip, snip, snip.

I have her knees, knobby and square;
and her skin, fair and raw
like the white meat of an apple
with a peel-able red casing.

I stay out of direct sunlight,
no longer believing that burnt skin
turns to a sylphlike tan.
Between suburb and city
lies an eternity that we barely acknowledge.

News

There are moments of habit that simply disappear
because life changes; like putting on your sneakers
and sweater and racing to the newsstand at 96th and Broadway
to get tomorrow's paper when it drops from
the truck at 11 pm. The traffic from the final hour
of the day still swirling down and up town. You place
the news, folded, underneath your arm as you go back home
to read about tomorrow—a splash of brandy near the laid-out
print, some Coltrane in the background on the radio. It wasn't
that life was simpler just these few decades ago. No,
that wasn't it. But the dexterity of the touch: the paper
under the arm, your hand on the doorknob way past dark,
a walk down Broadway not knowing what you would discover
and then, the infinite hours of sleep before conversation.

The Ed Sullivan Show

There was that crack of dusk, especially in springtime,
when the weekend melted into the other side of Monday
and the Ed Sullivan Show resounded through the house.

My brother and I—still damp from our baths,
our dripping heads smelling of Johnson's
Baby Shampoo—sat on the plush rug with our backs
against the blue Knoll sofa. Our pajamas with that lingering smell
that never dissipated, tickling our nostrils like the foam
on the lid of the fabric softener.

A long line of comics and rock stars file
through my memory as a parade on TV
in all their black and white splendor: The Beatles
and Herman's Hermits. . . Phyllis Diller, David Steinberg,
Joan Rivers, Rodney Dangerfield, and a comic—unnamable—
I dated just a few years ago.

No longer a boy wonder, but a gray-haired somewhat cranky companion,
he showed me boxes of framed photos with personalities too young
to have been on Sullivan like Sandra ("Sandy") Bullock and others I forgot.

He took me to the Friars' Club for lunch with a menu
of Chow Mein and Matzo Brei, a Catskills' special
enjoyed only by old Jews and usually before 6 o'clock at night.
The tables peopled by Borscht Belt comics I didn't know
and one famous TV star who sat across from his poodle.
They were both extremely thin and wired.

Before kissing me goodbye, he said, "I think that went well,"
like an audition. The world seemed oddly limited despite
the marquee names appearing before me in living color.
I wasn't sure how to redirect my dreams or where they would land or live.

I saw him again recently, at a funeral for the father of a mutual friend,
where I recited *Kaddish* on the *bimah* on behalf of the family
and he told jokes in a chapel filled with other stars from Sullivan,
their bodies aided by walkers and wheelchairs.

My red suede Manolo shoes, their three-inch heels so binding
that I had to discard them, go barefoot on the concrete street
in a world where all the lights on Broadway
couldn't compare to the imagination of one suburban household
and a black and white TV on Sunday night in 1966.

Cocktails in Warsaw, 2019

Is it too obvious to write: God is crying?
The rain falls in torrents from the Warsaw sky.
I sit with Israeli friends at a wine bar
under a canopy while tears drip through the slots.
Three black cars with flashing lights speed by
then slow down. The President is home
next door in his castle. The city breathes
with a busy modernity while the country
gets pushed and pulled like an accordion
between past and present, truth and lies.

Yes. God is crying, for sure,
watering the graves that lie under every stone.
Corpses gaze up at us through the smothered, buried earth.

I ask my taxi driver to take a detour past Mila 18.
The rain breaks as Orthodox schoolgirls from Israel
gab and flit on the sidewalk near the mound of grass,
oblivious to the burial place of the young and godless heroes.
Mordechai Anielewicz is a street in the ghetto
framed by emptiness and Soviet style apartment blocks.

There is nothing for God to do but to water the earth,
make it blossom again, touch our shoulders with
the fresh green smell of summertime
in a world as imperfect as ever.

Birkenau

The Haredi girl from Tiberias clutches
her *Siddur*, head buried, lips
move silently. She sways slightly,
couched in the back of her group,
seated outside, under the slim
and deceptively calming trees.

Like the others, she carries
a plastic bag of Glatt Kosher food.
My guide tells me he saw some
of the girls sneak away to
Ben & Jerry's at the concession stand.

I didn't know which shoes to wear,
to graze the hallowed and grieving ground.
So, I bought a new pair—rubber sandals
with a slide-through buckle—
for $30 in Krakow's Old Town.

I couldn't throw them out
afterwards, as I had planned.
They are in my closet, wrapped
in plastic. It wasn't the mounds
of shoes behind glass in the Auschwitz
Museum that took my breath;
but rather, the soft tread of the grass
and the mud and pebbles
near the train tracks, the mixing
of earth and history, dirt packed
for decades with shards of bone.

In Lviv

In Market Square, Putin's face is on
toilet paper and floor mats for sale
among the coffee and tomatoes.
In the park at dusk, I sit on a bench
pretending it's Lemberg before the war.
My full skirt scrapes the immaculate ground.
At the end of the road, the national gallery
gleams with a banner hailing the Ukrainian
prisoners of conscience locked up by Russia.

Stuck in the pages of Joseph Roth or Sholom Aleichem,
reversing in time to find something to hold in the present,
I am alone on a vast continent.

A tour guide takes me through streets
where so many Jews once lived. In a pocket
park, a stone is inscribed to the domed synagogue
burned to the ground as congregants, held back
by the Nazis, tried to run into the flames
to save the Torah scrolls.

Back at the Leopolis Hotel, I sit at the bar on a
night too drenched with rain to go outside.
The bartender, pale with red lipstick, speaks
perfect English that she learned in hipster Williamsburg.
She wants to return to Brooklyn or just America.
At the table next to me, a man from Copenhagen,
newly divorced, anxiously grips
a guidebook. Unburdened by history, he is
relieved to be anywhere but Denmark.

Travelog

I sit in the outdoor wine bar at the Bristol hotel
drinking a terrible Polish red.

The Warsaw Pact was signed in the white presidential palace next door
bringing drab grayness to the city for decades too sad to count.

Now, the sun is poised in a corner of the sky.
The cold of late summer waves below.

Tourists pass the palace while men in black suits and skinny ties
wait outside their luxury cars in the new Poland.

Democracy is hiding behind a ragged mass of clouds.

Earlier today, I walked the Royal Route past the University
with the plaque proclaiming support for '68.

In the Inglot make-up store, I sampled white nail enamel
and concealer for the dark circles that travel with me everywhere.

My ancestors lived somewhere in this country
when it was Poland and when it was Ukraine.

Galicianers, who fought for the emperor until the empire fought back,
they packed their things for an America they didn't know and couldn't imagine.

2019, Warsaw

No Matter

No matter how long I search
I will never find them, the ancestors—
the limbs that stretch
into the earth of Galicia—now Ukraine and Poland,
liquid maps drawn and redrawn.
The jumble of names misspelled.

They worked at simple jobs: shoe cobbler,
locksmith. And lamplighter—a great-great
grandfather who passed through the village at dusk
to light the wicks until the roads
were ribbons of white. One day I sat

in a park in Lviv surrounded by foreign
trees and children playing, imagining
the thick ankles and sturdy arms
of my great grandmothers like the trunks
of the maples along the path.

But it didn't matter. They were all gone
to America or to pogroms and Hitler,
disappeared into the dust of centuries.

Sunday in Gdansk

In the Gdansk inner harbor
the boat is filled with families and couples
toasting each other with pints.
The town becomes
only shipyards and then, the open sea.

A singer tests the microphone with his pointer finger.
Everyone else joins in. I am a kind of lonely
that is hard to feel or swallow.

We pass the shipyards, boats half-carcassed
where Solidarity was born,
converted into trendy loft living.
The Solidarity Museum has signage
on the glass doors at the entrance
proclaiming: "Europe begins here."

A light show about a people's revolution
reflects off the walls along the quay
as families enjoy ice cream cones. Lech Walesa
is in his apartment nearby, half-revered and half reviled.

In Westerplatte, on the tiny beach next to the parking lot
shirtless truck drivers stand near their rigs, their shorts
damp with the smell of land that sits awkwardly
between East and West. Here is a french fries stand
where the world once broke apart.

Whoever visits history gets to write it.

In the Kinneret Cemetery

Whither shall I go from the spirit?
—Psalms

In this country, even the ghosts have ghosts.
Here, the dead hold national congresses—
Moses Hess, Nachman Syrkin,
Ber Borochov, and lonely Rachel:
thrown from her perfect landswell.
What good was a poet with poisoned lungs
in a land where revolutionaries were farmers,
dreamers of a modern-day Eden?

O Rachel:
tell the seekers who drop pebbles
on your headstone, who sit between
your spirit and the water, who read
from the pages of your verse
stored in a vault by the sea.
Say what will become of us.
What will we become?

Burning Bush

The crop plane swept
close to the tree line
spraying the fire.
Orange flames danced near
the highway, then jumped back
across the Shoresh forest.

There was no Moses to stare down the burning bush,
only fire trucks stuck
in the back of a traffic lane
that stretched all the way to Ben Gurion.
Sirens whirred, but nothing moved.

The night before, I drove
on the Jerusalem Forest Road.
The only lights were my car's
single beam and a solo orange flame
rising between two picnic tables
where Haredi families ate.

The blooming orange flower pointed
toward the sky, as if
the picnickers were testing God.

The flame's embers slept
with one eye open, awaiting the dawn,
feeding on the drought and extreme
heat of a July desert summer.

Now, the orange is ash and brown
on a broken, windswept gateway
to the city of imagined miracles.

In Case the Messiah Comes

Split screen city.
East doesn't go West
and West doesn't go East.
Occupied neighborhoods,
buildings on buildings on dust of history.

Ramat Shlomo Haredi new homes
with their backside to Shuafat.
The red brick headquarters model
of 770 Eastern Parkway rising
amid the white stone—in case
the Messiah comes and wants
to live a short walk from a refugee camp.

The innocent Judean hills,
their grape essence, unkosher wineries
threaded between the rabbis' blessed canisters.
Here is what it takes to make wine kosher:
only Jewish hands can touch the grape to the bottle.
It seems an unholy use of God—to separate
us from the fields to the label.

Back in the neighborhoods, busy
ramps coming and going from Route 1
and 443—sometimes you can tell
from the car who is who
without glancing inside, but
other times, not at all.
There is no union here.

No common language.
The clogged *tzomet*, junction
East-West veers forward
and backward. The light rail
like a careening snake
moving back and forth,
like a traveling steel pendulum
striking at the rubble of centuries
and the messiah's endless climb.

Destinations

Why is it that the memory my mind chose
to find today is of a time
when the flights to Israel
were invisible on European destination boards?
In Paris
or London
or Amsterdam
or Frankfurt
the flight to TLV
read "see the desk."

So I did, always to find
a number for a door that led
to a bus that stood waiting
to take the passengers
to a far end of the runway
to an El Al airliner
lonely and empty.
Its white and blue carcass
there in full blaze
on a steamy runway
with a European cityscape behind it:
read Paris
or London
or Amsterdam
or Frankfurt.

It was like flying
without a destination,
although assuming
I would always arrive in Tel Aviv
in the old airport, too stuffed
for the arrivals, bulged with people and luggage,
Haredi women pushing,
chasing *sheitel* boxes and puffed-up
suitcases tied with ribbon going round
and round and round in the terminal.

When the kids were little,
we would drive through pebbly fields
near the moshav, searching
for pomegranate fruit on the trees.
My cousin stopped the truck by the road
to take each child by the hand leading
her and then him, into the bushes,
a sweaty roll of toilet paper packed
into a knapsack pocket.
Later, we ate cheese and fresh lettuces
with carafes of wine
and tiny bowls of jelly and butter
at the goat farm on the ridge.
At night, the lights from the Arab villages
lit up like pearls on oyster beds,
the dark green silt of the countryside
leading us back home.

Once, I drove the length of the border
along the north, from Kiryat Shmona to Achziv.
The tanks were napping alongside the fence.
Dust overtook the green. The road was skinny, steep, empty
of civilians. I sped, with the music of *Galei Tzahal*
refracting like tin bumps inside the car.
I knew where I was, in a manner of speaking.
I had only to drive a straight line
in this contained part of the universe,
on the cusp of war, at the cusp of Hezbollah
with the tanks belching out their tiredness,
as Shabbat began for the Jews
and Sabbath ended for the Muslims
living in separate clusters along the roadside.

Route 443

White vans parked by the sides, checkpoints,
and a feeble bridge reinforced
with electronic eyes across the upper rim.
This road is a river that separates
the flow of Israel from a non-Palestine.

Villages line the banks, home to what seems
like an endless supply of workers, but really full
of men (mostly) who rise at dawn to cross
to earn to feed their families. Each person
has a story, birth date and his/her
hours running down.

A very human task made less
than human. White vans
like floating sails on the asphalt delivering
day laborers to build, to cook, to clean.
In darkness, they are empty hulks asleep,
waiting for their passengers.

From there, the navigation directs me
to Atarot, where factories sit
atop the cliffed edge of the West Bank.
White apartment bloc buildings. Transport trucks parked
outside, their drivers asleep before morning haul.
No signs in Hebrew. Just servants doing tasks.

From the back side streets,
emptying onto Nablus
Road, Beit Hanina, music
of lights and flares, signs
point to the City Center, to a Jerusalem
without a true center, many centers, too many gods.

On the Day after Christmas

On the day after Christmas, I went to Bethlehem
to see the celebration that lingered past the holiday.
The sheep in Beit Sahour were grazing in a dirty lot
between two steep hills. And the blonde ponytail
of the Israeli soldier flapped in the wind between the barrier
near a jeep outfitted like a monster with grids of black
protective gear all over it: a mask, a shield—
so that this jeep was almost like a tank,
a difficult dancer on the hills that barely stretch
from Jerusalem to this birth city, a literal stone's throw
popping from one holy name to the next,
Jerusalem-Bethlehem-Bethlehem-Jerusalem.

Oh, the traffic jams, to get into the city, to get out,
the grey cement wall snaking and standing.
There were crowds at the falafel stand and bowls
of hummus with whole chickpeas at the edge of Manger Square.
Good Shepherd Beer for sale next to cotton candy.
A green synthetic tree with red lights stretching
above the landscape, tourists reaching backwards
and forwards with no guidebook, only the dumb sheep
in the city lot, and the hills, wet with the winter rains
and the smell of green.

Time Zones

i.

My eyes are asking me to stop writing,
you tell me. It's 3 am your time. Here
in Brooklyn, I am flipping through your messages
on my iPhone—half in English, half in Arabic (which I don't understand).
We talk ISIS, Adonis, and the utility of Google Translate.

ii.

On a dark January day in Jerusalem
I sip red wine, cupping the glass in memory
of Darwish and his studious intensity
toward the red liquid.
Your whiskey glass
sits in a puddle of feint water on the table
near my computer. Christian pilgrims
hug their teacups close where they sit behind us.
Arabic is good for speaking between the lines.

iii.

Adonis reads his poems about Jerusalem
at the French cultural center on Fifth Avenue,
where spring pours in from the wide windows.
"In art, there is no East and West,"
he quips. "Religion is an answer and poetry
is a question." But I can't help leaving

the reading with a question: how did Syria
not seep into that precious room,
with the wooden beams and the delicate
hanging light fixtures?

Who are we, poets
and fans, to push the essence of the war
away from our faces, out of our minds,
even for an hour as we praise metaphor
over answers? Even asking a question is enough—
an important beginning, but not to ask,
to stay silent, that, too, is a type of metaphor
or a simile: silence is like. . .
Silence is like the breath before death,
the gasp unheard.

iv.

There is that whisper of days when Jerusalem
 becomes two time zones
and sunset happens twice.
You can run from West to East
and add an hour to your life
for just two days a year when East Jerusalemites
join their clock hands to the people on the other side
of Qalandia, Hizmeh, the DCL, and lag a day behind
official Israel's daylight savings shift. A silent rebellion
that separates neighborhoods or something else?
The warm moon smiles down on the silly people
who are unable to synchronize the hours
as the mash of wild rosemary and chickweed
aim to stretch toward daylight.

Nighttime in Jericho

Sometimes an evening with friends
begins so simply that the geopolitics
disappear at least through cocktails.
On this winter night in Jericho—eight days
into the new year, a still and temperate dark night—
we gather outside near the backyard pool
with blankets and hookahs, wine goblets
stained in a deep red.

There are no checkpoints to enter Jericho,
just two tired Palestinian guards
seated on the side of the road;
the empty casino with its gigantic promise
of cross-border commerce and hijinks
on one side and a Palestinian
prison on the other. The quiet coffee shops
line up as we drive to the end of town
where the vacation villas are,
to eat and drink, amid ouds and tiny drums.

But by dessert, when the Arak flows
and the dinner that began near midnight becomes
a sleepy pre-dawn offering, the storytelling
and laughter mutate into a fury not found
elsewhere on this vast globe.

We look around the room—
pick out the fortunate ones:
a Spanish journalist, me—the American Jew from Brooklyn,
a Tel Avivi musician and then, the rest,
who return home to Beit Hanina,
the neighborhood without passports.

There is that time in the evening, always
when the toasts are finished and the light touch
on the knee, friend to friend, snaps apart
like the broken head of a doll;
when the wine stops flowing and the motors
start up. Everyone returns to their corners
in this endless fight, not simply for survival,
but for its gilded lining.

Snow Day

I sit in a dark Brooklyn living room waiting for midnight to arrive.
The phone against my ear is the only light.
For you, it's five am. We talk until your sun comes up.
With my feet lodged on the sofa rim, I close my eyes
to let your voice transport me to Jerusalem.

Now, daylight on the streets of Sheikh Jarrah, the British
Consulate turning light next to the Swedes and the empty
hotels. The amber and fuchsia color of sunrise rims
the darkness in my eyes.

You make coffee, the terrible instant stuff
that floats in your cup as you sit
at the kitchen table with your first cigarette.
You're wearing a scarf with your pajamas
to stay warm against the Jerusalem chill
like an anxious schoolboy
waiting for his first winter snow.

The sun rises over the buildings farther east.
It's a hole in the sky, you tell me, as you turn
your iPhone to show me the crisp yellow air
outside your white windows. The sky surrounding
the yellow hole is a shade of gray, like our moods,
in this, our pandemic lives.

Still, there is no snow to show me.
We synchronized our body clocks so that now
it's Wednesday for both of us. My day begins
with sleep. You will finish your cigarette
and practice your oud. The hole in the sky
remains. That strip of yellow that holds everything
in our irregular lives continents apart, time zones,
darkness bleeding into light and then back again.
All of the airplanes in the world have stopped flying.
The dark apartment gets darker as my eyes adjust
to the absence. The hours roll forward—
You, to your morning and me, toward sleep.
But really, time has simply stopped. That thing
that makes us rise each morning to discover
something unimagined or untried is stuck
in place. The planes have stopped flying
and the sirens are terrifying lullabies.

Remembering Marrakesh

It came to me as an aroma, the smell of men
and coffee, and sky, oh—and traffic. The fumes
of male bodies and the exhaust of cars.
I was tired from walking the streets of Gueliz
after shopping and the Majorelle, and I wanted
coffee, but only men sat in the cafés.
I was confused. Could I sit down according to local custom
to have coffee at a sidewalk café on Avenue Mohammed V?

Finally, after pacing back and forth on the block, with no one
to ask, I decided to sit in a café alone, but inside, where I saw
women seated laughing and drinking alongside men.
Even so, many years later, I wonder, could I have seated myself
outside among the sea of men smoking and drinking their coffee?
Would the world have erupted or would it remain exactly the same?
Me, returning just days later via Casablanca to New York, weighted
down with rugs I didn't need, but that make me smile each time I enter my
apartment and step on them, one by one, first one and then the other.

That smell of coffee and men, men and coffee, and cigarettes
—the smell that populates the Arab street. I wanted to sit alone
outside in the café among the sea of men, but something
inside of me said, no no, inside is better, ensconced in the warm winter heat
on the other side of the sidewalk, beyond the glass
partitions and the men sitting, smoking, their leather jackets
soaking up the smell of tobacco and the sweet aroma
of coffee on a warm winter's day in Gueliz.

Mill Hands

i.

In Cairo on the Giza Road, we see factories
stacked side by side with girls and boys as young as six
on the looms, their tiny fingers like precious ingots,
as they thread the silk, seated but not at rest.
Beefier boys on standing looms shift the spindles
back and forth, back, and forth like extra arms.

"Technical schools," our tour guide calls them.
She whispers to the floor manager, calculates
her cut in potential sales, denies these kids—
smiley and sparkly for our cameras—
are missing school, while someone
from our group bargains for a rug,
unswayed by our shaming. "Cultural relativism,"
this person smirks.

Just down the road, the pyramids bake
in the sun, the sand around them littered
with camel dung and empty cigarette packs.
Boys chase after us. "Picture with a camel, lady?"
These ageless limestone excavations with ghostly skeletons
lie back and sunbathe through the centuries
while tourists smear sunscreen on their noses.

ii.

In Opelika, Alabama, grown workers
were called mill hands by their bosses,
as if their hands were simply stand alones
without mind or spirit or wearied feet,
reduced to the part of them that earns
not much, but enough to get by.
When the Hollywood crew came
on sight to make *Norma Rae*, the workers
were extras on their own shop floor.
Sally Field portrayed the activist
seduced to the cause by Reuben
Warshovski, the fictional organizer.

Mothers beside daughters beside granddaughters
beside grandfathers beside fathers beside sons.
It stayed like that until the Piedmont
emptied of spindles and looms.
Now the factory floors that once sweated as high
as 100 degrees, while the wilting workers imagined
a river like the Nile flowing outside their heavy windows,
are frozen still. The mill's been shut for good.
The buildings sit—random and rusted,
a poor excuse for pyramids,
while the cement sinks in place and withers.

Praying to God on the Subway

The woman seated next to me prays
to her iPhone. The Hebrew script: *Baruch, Atah, Adonoi,*
disappears as she scrolls down. I watch her lips
move to the sync of the words, her stiff auburn *sheitel*
grazes her shoulders. The heavy, but stylish,
stockings are odd, but necessary for her
in this heat and in her way, in this New York City,
in this Brooklyn, in this subway.
I watch her pray. She won't
look at me even once.
She could turn to me and say:
Please, some privacy, I am here with God.

But, instead, she ignores the life all around her:
A tattooed young woman with purple hair,
a mother and her two-year old scrambling
to climb from his stroller, a construction worker,
shining with the dusty film of a building rising.
This is the busy earth and
the down-underbelly of New York.
Her lips move so quickly that her teeth
disappear. No matter how hard I try
I will never be as certain as she,
unmindful of all except for
the holy one, blessed is he.

Isaac's Story

When we reached the top I asked:
"Where is the ram?"
"Wait, my son, it will appear," he whispered.
But our hands separated. He strapped
me to the altar. My bones
hugged the cold wood. The rope
chafed against my shoulders.

What could I do,
flesh of his flesh?
I walk in his shadow,
rise, fall in his shadow.

Yet, even harnessed to the altar,
my eyes saw more clearly.
my throat gave breath more easily.
my youth urged him onward.

I cried: "Father—" my words
eclipsed in the roar from above.
His hand slipped as my brother
the ram appeared.
We roasted the ram, but

The smoke could not hide the weakness
in my father's arms when he tried
to comfort me, hold me. His eyes
filled with tears; an aged servant
at God's mercy, his son's mercy.

There is no solace in knowing
the workings of this world.

Dressing for My Father's Funeral

Worm, be with me.
This is my hard time.

—Theodore Roethke

What if I forget my shoes
and let the mud around
your newly dug grave
suck in my feet like suction?

I lay a row of pearls
against my neck bone
to keep out the cold
on the journey without
minutes or hours or days or years.

O Son of Samuel,
between night and day,
there is a precise chaos
that we, the living,
must endure.

If God Could

If God could return all those years
when we sat outside or upstairs or behind
a barrier, when we shouted but no one heard,
when we prayed but our prayers were dismissed,
when the white silk of the *tallit* was kept
from our shoulders and we covered our arms
instead with our best jackets and dresses from Bonwit's.

We hugged our prayers to our hearts in silence.

If God could, but never mind.
We need no one's permission—not even God's.
The sanctuary is full of women and children.
The rabbi leads us—
our voices, loud and whispering.
Her voice, trilling with the empty decades.

O God of our fathers and mothers
O God of our sons and daughters
O God of our grandmothers, we gather
all the silenced voices in a circle.
The sanctuary is full like never before,
full with the union of every voice.

Psalm 15

after David's psalm

God, who may join you in your shelter?

This is who:
She walks blameless and creates justice.
She speaks truth in her heart.
She doesn't have a loose tongue
or do evil to another.
She never disgraces someone close to her.

In her eyes, an evil actor is despised.
She honors God, treating this presence
with the reverence reserved only for holiness.

She keeps her promises, even if it means losing money.
She can't be bribed. She is unbending.

Who may join you in your shelter?
Someone who creates heaven on earth,
who lives without fear of death,
knowing how she has spent her time;
knowing that her shelter is filled
with the music and poetry of those
who came before.

Resplendency

My hands fold at my third eye.
I get ready to sprint, to dive
into Down Dog, Up Dog.
Urdha mukha svanasana
Adho mukha svanasana.
This learning a new language.
My mat is a tiny room.

The fumes of others
surround me. Their much
younger bodies folded
like pipe cleaners
that I played with
as a kid—before
all of them were born.
They are resplendent
in wheels and headstands,
while I nearly topple
becoming a tree.

My core
is a tiny sea
of waves. I force
my muscle to wrap
around my bones
and my fat
like a corset.
Warrior Three,
I tip my body
and my hands
leave the floor.

My torso,
like a cup without
a handle. Inhaling
my flesh, my bone,
my muscle,
I whisper
a prayer to some god
somewhere in a svelte
oratory of sweat.

Then, Sphinx pose.
Shavassana
Shavassana
Shavassana,
as if my breath
is a string, a song
leading me to these
last decades in
resplendent motion.

Hudson

The only ice cream parlor opened
on the Friday night before Labor Day
is in Hudson. So, we drive
from Old Chatham to the main street
in this once suffering town, embraced
now by Brooklyn hipsters.
The ice cream store sells
kefir ice cream, a sour milk—some sort
of testament to health or coolness.

Outdoor human-made coverings
along the empty street that popped up
during Covid to feed us and shelter us
from the plague, like out of season *Sukkas*.

It's a mystery I can't resolve:
why are the streets that dot
this adorable, quaint pocket of commerce
in the farmland countryside so empty?
Is everyone at home in their yards
eating with family over picnic tables or in gardens
with an overload of tomatoes that tumbled
to the ground, waiting for deer to pick at
or an enthusiastic weekend guest to gather
and simmer into tomato sauce for the colder months?

Or are they in dark forests
behind the houses that skim the street front
seated around crude bonfires
like we were last night as we tried
to name all the constellations,
but got stuck gazing at Venus, since
its brightness outshone the entire open sky.

Sour milk ice cream must be the oddest invention,
unnecessary, almost spiteful. But we eat it anyway
because there are no other options.

We have been friends for nearly half a century.
At age 16, in summer camp we drank icy milk
and ate oversized chocolate chip cookies.

We had an abundance of dreams back then, probably
never thinking about driving through the summer night
—two frantic old ladies in search of ice cream in the hills
of upstate New York, the light of Venus now obscured
by a night sky, heavy with clouds along streets, empty
of the very people they were designed to entertain.

Uncoupled

It rained for 40 days and 40 nights.
The couples walked up the plank
to the ark. I stood outside, uncertain
how to ascend; uncoupled, unhooked,
a lone woman, my feet soaked from
the sagging earth.

The waters surged above the sidewalk.
My body half-immersed in the storm
water, like a warm, but dirty bath.
No one grabbed my hand. No one
embraced me as the waters rose.
Then, I saw the horizon ripple through the waves.

Adornment

On my first trip to Paris I bought a
multi-colored scarf—violet with blueberries—
for my mother who left it on a barstool at the Bluebell Inn.
She was there to pick up men.

I gave her the violet and blueberry scarf
and she wore it once or twice, perhaps.
She went to pick up men and left it
on a barstool, when she was giggling with her girlfriends.

She wore it once or twice, perhaps
as she dressed in outfits distinct from her past
on a barstool, giggling with her girlfriends.
She tried to be the carefree widow.

I bought her a scarf on my first trip to Paris.
It's that scarf I see as she tucks her napkin in her sweater
to soak up the tomato sauce—across from me in the restaurant.
Her once high cheekbones are sagging

as she sits back in her chair. To where did the inches disappear?
I see her now in me as I stare in the mirror. She wore it
once or twice perhaps—and all the other things she gave me—
a Beged-Or suede jacket, now more than fifty years old.

She was so beautiful. But when I look into the mirror
I see her sagging cheekbones and I feel inches fly from beneath
my feet. Maybe the mirror lies. Memories, too. I try
to contain the love as I grasp a diamond locket

around my neck. From her mother to mine, to me.
They are dead and I adorn myself with these bits
of memory. I gave her the violet and blueberry scarf
and remember it as if it were yesterday.

Then and Now

We bought me black snow boots from a market vendor in the 5th.
I insisted on moving from our hotel with the toilet in the hallway.
You photographed me shivering outside the Pantheon,
my scarf wrapped tightly like a blanket.
I was so young. I couldn't imagine
what sixty would look like—or seventy—or. . .
Now, in the store windows, my face is long.
My eyes have pockets.

You are a shadow behind me, the broad girth
of your imaginary body, your thick white hair.
Sunglasses—oh god, I can't remember
the color of your eyes. But I feel your stubborn—
or steady—presence along the sidewalk,
crossing the street, in my hotel room,
at a bar, everywhere, everywhere.

There were socialists back then. You left me
alone to meet Chevènement for lunch.
Now, Solferino is mannerless, a fancy dress shop
sits near the old party headquarters.
We walk along the Seine. I try to hide
our conversation, covering my mouth
so that no one sees me talking to myself, to you,
to our years.

The Ladder

"I am not done with my changes."
—Stanley Kunitz

Eventually, as I climb the rungs through my sixties,
time becomes nominal. It's about racing and slowing
down. Intentionally and forced.
Some days I see my reflection and it's not me.

Time becomes nominal. It's about racing and slowing.
There's a shadow on the mirror.
It's my mother, or a stranger with lines
from my forehead to my neck.

There's a shadow on the mirror.
I see myself like always, whatever
always is—a make-believe reflection of agelessness.
But then, my knees remind me:

I see myself. The up and down of everyday
defeats me like it never did before.
These quartets of pain hobble me into a cocoon,
backwards into childhood as I venture up the rungs.

NOTES

Cocktails in Warsaw

The President is home: The president of Poland lives in an old castle next to the Bristol Hotel and Wine Bar. When this poem was written, the current Law and Justice ruling party was attempting to rewrite some major facts of Polish history and control the media.

Mordechai Anielewicz: A socialist-Zionist leader of the Hashomer Hatzair youth movement in Poland, and head of the Jewish Fighting Organization that led the Warsaw Ghetto Uprising, in which he and most of his comrades died. Mila 18 was the street address where they lived in the ghetto, now a memorial as a mound of grass.

Birkenau

Siddur: A prayerbook, Hebrew.

In the Kinneret Cemetery

The names in this poem were left-wing founders of Israel, including Rachel, who became a national poet, though she was asked to leave her kibbutz. All are buried in the Kinneret Cemetery overlooking the Kinneret (Lake Galilee).

In Case the Messiah Comes

Ramat Shlomo: A new neighborhood for Lubavitcher Haredi (ultra-Orthodox) Jews built on land by Israel adjoining Palestinian neighborhoods in East Jerusalem and an expansive Palestinian refugee camp (Shuafat). The Lubavitcher Hasidim believe that their founder, Menachem Schneerson, is the Messiah, and they build replicas of their Brooklyn brick-faced headquarters wherever they are, in case Schneerson, upon a re-emergence, wants to feel at home in any of their enclaves.

Destinations

Sheitel: A wig box, Hebrew/Yiddish.

Moshav: Once cooperative communities, now tiny suburbs.

Galei Tzahal: An Israeli radio station.

Route 443

Route 443: Sometimes called "the apartheid road," not only by Palestinians, but also by Jewish Israeli peace activists. It meanders through Palestinian occupied territory as well as Israel proper, with an electronic checkpoint in the middle of it and some travel restrictions for Palestinians.

Atarot and *Beit Hanina:* East Jerusalem Palestinian neighborhoods.

Just servants doing tasks: Joshua, chapter 16, mentions Caananites dwelling among the Hebrews to 'do taskwork.'

Time Zones

Time Zones: East Jerusalem Palestinian population and West Bank Palestinians usually conform to Jordanian daylight savings protocol, while Israel adheres to its own protocol—so there is a brief time when East and West Jerusalem essentially live in two different time zones.

Qalandia, Hizmeh, the DCL: Israeli Defense Force checkpoints between the West Bank, Occupied Palestinian territory, and Israel.

Nighttime in Jericho

Beit Hanina: A neighborhood in East Jerusalem with a Palestinian population, many of whom don't have passports as they are considered stateless.

If God Could

Tallit: A prayer shawl, historically worn just by men. Until 1973, women in liberal Judaism could not be rabbis. This poem was written for a 50-year commemoration of women rabbis.

Hudson

Sukkas: Booths erected outside for the Jewish festival of Sukkoth.

Then and Now

Chevènement: A leftwing minister in the Mitterand government in France.

Solferino: A street in the 7th Arrondissement, and also the former Socialist Party headquarters when the Socialists ran the government.

ACKNOWLEDGEMENTS

The author would like to thank the following publications in which these poems first appeared:

Cocktails in Warsaw, 2019, Time Zones, Nighttime in Jericho, Route 443: Atlanta Review (*Cocktails in Warsaw* and *Time Zones* won international poetry awards)

If God Could: An anthology honoring 50 years of women in the Reform rabbinate, published by Central Conference of American Rabbis (CCAR) Press

In the Kinneret Cemetery: Anthology, *Without a Single Answer: Poems on Contemporary Israel,* published by Judah Magnes Museum

On the Day After Christmas: Upstreet Journal

In Mostar, City of Bridges: Plume Poetry Anthology #6

Market Day, Summer circa 1967-2xxx, Destinations, In Case the Messiah Comes, Sunday in Gdansk: Plume Poetry

Paris, How She Remembers Him, Remembering Marrakech, Adornment: Stand, UK

Not in This Lifetime: Women's Review of Books & adapted with lyrics by Hillary Rollins & music by Michelle Brourman for the song "My Daughters"

In Lviv: Given honorable mention in Other Voices Israel, on their website and print anthology

Photo by Adam Lempel

Jo-Ann Mort returned to poetry writing when she turned 60. Her poetry has appeared recently in *Plume, UpStreet, Stand* (UK), *the Atlanta Review*, and elsewhere. A 1978 graduate of Sarah Lawrence College, she also did graduate work in poetry and philosophy at NYU.

Her previous lives inform her poetry, as do her global wanderings—as a trade union activist, a political organizer, and a long time advocate for, and writer about, peace between Israelis and Palestinians. Jo-Ann has written analysis and reported for more than 40 years from Israel and the Occupied Palestinian Territories (OPT), including the West Bank and Gaza. Her journalism is widely published in the US and UK. Jo-Ann is a member of the national steering committee of Writers for Democratic Action.

Born and raised in Lafayette Hill, Pennsylvania, she is a longtime resident of Park Slope, Brooklyn.

Books by

ARROWSMITH

PRESS

Fifty-Two by Melissa Green

Music In—And On—The Air by Lloyd Schwartz

Magpiety by Melissa Green

Reality Hunger by William Pierce

Soundings: On The Poetry of Melissa Green
edited by Sumita Chakraborty

The Corny Toys by Thomas Sayers Ellis

Black Ops by Martin Edmunds

Museum of Silence by Romeo Oriogun

City of Water by Mitch Manning

Passeggiate by Judith Baumel

Persephone Blues by Oksana Lutsyshyna

The Uncollected Delmore Schwartz
edited by Ben Mazer

The Light Outside by George Kovach

The Blood of San Gennaro by Scott Harney
edited by Megan Marshall

No Sign by Peter Balakian

Firebird by Kythe Heller

The Selected Poems of Oksana Zabuzhko
edited by Askold Melnyczuk

cont...

The Age of Waiting by Douglas J. Penick

Manimal Woe by Fanny Howe

Crank Shaped Notes by Thomas Sayers Ellis

The Land of Mild Light by Rafael Cadenas
edited by Nidia Hernández

The Silence of Your Name: The Afterlife of a Suicide by Alexandra Marshall

Flame in a Stable by Martin Edmunds

Mrs. Schmetterling by Robin Davidson

This Costly Season by John Okrent

Thorny by Judith Baumel

The Invisible Borders of Time: Five Female Latin American Poets
edited by Nidia Hernández

Some of You Will Know by David Rivard

The Forbidden Door: The Selected Poetry of Lasse Söderberg
tr. by Lars Gustaf Andersson & Carolyn Forché

Unrevolutionary Times by Houman Harouni

Between Fury & Peace: The Many Arts of Derek Walcott
edited by Askold Melnyczuk

The Burning World by Sherod Santos

Today is a Different War: Poetry of Lyudmyla Khersonska
tr. by Olga Livshin, Andrew Janco, Maya Chhabra, & Lev Fridman

ARROWSMITH is named after the late William Arrowsmith, a renowned classics scholar, literary and film critic. General editor of thirty-three volumes of *The Greek Tragedy in New Translations*, he was also a brilliant translator of Eugenio Montale, Cesare Pavese, and others. Arrowsmith, who taught for years in Boston University's University Professors Program, championed not only the classics and the finest in contemporary literature, he was also passionate about the importance of recognizing the translator's role in bringing the original work to life in a new language.

Like the arrowsmith who turns his arrows straight and true, a wise person makes his character straight and true.

— Buddha